W9-BMP-970

COLORS

of the Rain Forest

by Elizabeth Bennett

SCHOLASTIC INC.

Some frogs in the rain forest have **RED** eyes.

This tree frog uses its bright eyes to scare away predators.

This chameleon
has an

ORANGE

tail.

―――――

Some chameleons
can change color
to blend into their
surroundings.

Watch out for the **YELLOW** snake!

This snake is called an eyelash viper. Can you guess why?

Can you find the

GREEN bug hiding on the **GREEN** leaf?

This bug is called a leaf katydid. It has strong legs for jumping and wings for flying.

BLUE poison dart frogs live in the rain forest.

They come in lots of colors, like yellow, orange, green, red, black, and blue.

This beetle has a

PURPLE

shell.

This type of beetle eats fungus, like mushrooms.

Can you name the COLORS in this bird's feathers?

This bird is named after all of its colors—it's a rainbow lorikeet!

TAKE A CLOSER LOOK!

COLORS

The **leaf katydid** looks like a leaf and blends right into its surroundings and fools its predators. There are two thousand different kinds of katydids in the Amazon rain forest.

The **red-eyed tree frog** uses its color for protection. Its green body helps it blend into its surroundings, and its bright red eyes scare some predators away!

The **poison dart frog** uses its bright colors to warn other animals to stay away. Some are blue like this one, but they can also be yellow, orange, green, red, or even black.

There are more than 160 different types of **chameleons**, and they come in a variety of colors including pink, blue, red, orange, turquoise, yellow, and green.

These tiny beetles are members of the fungus beetle family. Sometimes they are called **pleasing fungus beetles** because they are such pretty colors.

The **eyelash viper** is named for the scales above its eyes that look like eyelashes. Many of these snakes are yellow, but they can also be green or pink.

This beautiful bird is named after its color, or rather, all of its colors — it's a **rainbow lorikeet**!